MAKING CONNECTIONS
AMERICAN INDIANS AND SETTLERS

by Catherine DiMartino

Editorial Offices: Glenview, Illinois • Parsippany, New Jersey • New York, New York

Sales Offices: Needham, Massachusetts • Duluth, Georgia • Glenview, Illinois
Coppell, Texas • Sacramento, California • Mesa, Arizona

New Beginnings

When the European colonists came to North America, they settled a land with its own geography, history, and culture. The settlers had to change their way of life to survive in this land. There were already people living in this land, and these people were the American Indians, or Native Americans. The settlers and the American Indians had a very complicated relationship. Throughout early American history the settlers and American Indians fought wars against each other, made trade and military **alliances**, and shared numerous ideas.

The Thirteen English Colonies

The settlers, who were also called colonists, lived along the Atlantic coast of North America. There were thirteen colonies along this coast. Each colony was unique. However, the colonies that were geographically close to one another shared similar climates. The way each of the colonies was settled was based on these differences. As a result, there were three distinct colonial regions. The regions were called the New England, the Middle, and the Southern Colonies. The American Indians, who settled this land long before the arrival of the colonists, lived in groups whose lands consisted of more than one colony or region.

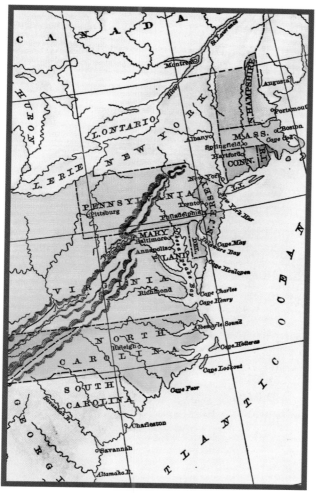

The Thirteen English Colonies

The New England Colonies

The New England Colonies had rocky soil, cold winters, and short summers. Because the soil in New England made it difficult to farm, a cash crop that could be grown and sold to markets was never developed. Most farmers in New England were **self-sufficient**. They grew just enough food to survive on, but not enough to sell to markets. The colonists learned important farming techniques, such as how to grow corn, from the American Indians.

Fishing, boat building, and trading were all important jobs that shaped the New England economy. The New England forests supplied lumber that could be used to build ships. Other natural resources present in New England were iron and animal furs. The colonists got furs by trading with American Indians.

Metacom, also known as "King Philip," led the Wampanoag in Kings Philip's War.

In 1633 Dutch colonists expanded their fur trade from the Hudson River valley in present-day New York State to present-day Connecticut. The English colonists in Massachusetts wanted to compete with the Dutch for the fur trade. The Pequot, a powerful American Indian group, saw the English as more of a threat than the Dutch. To fight the Pequot, the English made an alliance with the Mohegan and the Narragansett, rivals of the Pequot. In 1637 conflicts over land and the fur trade led to a war involving the English, the Pequot, the Mohegan, and the Narragansett. This was known as the Pequot War. In 1638 English colonists and their American Indian allies defeated the Pequot. Hundreds of Pequot were killed. For nearly forty years after the Pequot War ended, New England did not engage in any major conflicts with the American Indians.

In 1675 King Philip's War was the most destructive conflict between American Indians and the colonists up to that time. Twelve out of ninety New England towns were destroyed and 5 percent of the colonists were killed. Almost 40 percent of the American Indians were killed or fled the region. After the war, the American Indians who stayed in New England lived in small, scattered communities. The American Indians could not oppose the large groups of colonists. They lost control of their land, and by the 1700s English colonists started moving west.

The Middle Colonies

Unlike the New England Colonies, the Middle Colonies had a more moderate climate and soil that was very good for farming. The Middle Colonies grew wheat, barley, and oats, grains they traded with the other colonies. As a result, they were often called the "breadbasket" colonies.

There were fewer towns in the Middle Colonies than in New England because of the large amount of space that was required for farming. Instead of using land for a town square, as in New England, farmers in the Middle Colonies needed large areas of land to grow crops and raise animals. In addition, the Middle Colonies had excellent iron and coal resources and a strong fur industry. All of these were used for trade.

Because many of the colonists who lived in Massachusetts were Puritans, people who practiced other religious beliefs were persecuted. In contrast, the Middle Colonies had much more diversity and more religious freedom. Quakers, Presbyterians, Mennonites, and Catholics all lived in the Middle Colonies. The Quakers, many of whom lived in Pennsylvania, were known for their acceptance of other people, especially African Americans and American Indians.

In 1682 William Penn founded the Pennsylvania colony. That same year, he made a treaty with the Lenni Lenape group. In the treaty Penn promised to pay them for most of the land that King Charles had given him. Compared with many other colonies, Pennsylvania had no major conflicts with American Indians—at least throughout Penn's lifetime.

The Lenape, or Delaware, lived in a region that consisted of much of the Middle Colonies. In 1600 there were about twenty thousand Delaware. By 1700 their numbers decreased to about four thousand, due to several wars and disease. One cause of these wars was the fur trade between the American Indians and the European colonists. In order to meet the growing demand for fur, several American Indian groups competed for the same hunting territories. This competition led to war among the groups.

William Penn made a treaty with the Delaware in 1682.

The Southern Colonies

In the Southern Colonies, the winters were shorter and milder than in the other colonies. The geography was also different. The land along the Atlantic Coast was a mixture of bays, swamps, and rivers. This land was fertile and often wet, making it very good for growing tobacco, indigo, and rice. These crops were often grown on plantations. Large southern plantations had their own blacksmiths and dressmakers. In some cases large plantations had bigger populations than some towns in New England.

The crops grown by large plantations brought a lot of wealth to the southern colonies. Most southerners, however, did not own plantations. Many southerners were self-sufficient farmers, like the ones in New England. Some southerners lived in the **backcountry**, where there were dense woods and hills. People living in the backcountry had complicated relationships with the American Indians of that region, on whose hunting and fishing areas the colonists had settled.

American Indians known as the Tuscarora went to war against the North Carolina colonists in 1711. Two years later, the colonists defeated the Tuscarora with the help of the Yamasee, a rival American Indian group. In 1715 the Yamasee made an alliance with part of the Creek group in their own fight against the colonists. The colonists defeated this alliance with the help of the Cherokee and other American Indians. By the end of the war, the American Indians were defeated, and many of the survivors were driven from their homes to Spanish-held Florida.

From 1700 to 1715 more than a million animal furs were shipped from the port city of Charleston, South Carolina. The fur trade forced the Cherokee to hunt farther from their homes. Competition with the colonists for hunting grounds, wars with other American Indians, and disease were some of the challenges faced by the Cherokee. Between 1773 and 1792, the Cherokee signed several treaties that gave nearly all of their land in the South to the colonists.

This wood carved mask is an artifact of the Cherokee culture.

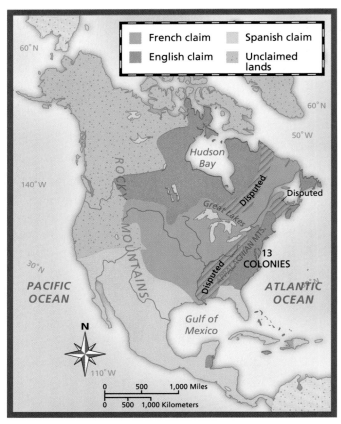

European Land Claims, 1750

The Ohio River Valley

The English, the French, and many different American Indian nations fought over land in North America. By the early 1700s the population along the Atlantic coast was growing rapidly. Some English colonists began to move west and cross the Appalachian Mountains for more land on which to settle. By the mid-1700s, many English colonists were moving into a region called the Ohio River valley.

This region was important because the Ohio River was a **tributary** of the Mississippi River. Both the French and the English wanted to control the Ohio River valley because of its access to the Mississippi River, fertile land, and its central location for trade. France had already claimed the Mississippi River and all of its tributaries as part of New France in the 1670s. The French had set up **trading posts** by the mid-1700s where they traded goods with American Indians. In addition, the American Indians wanted to protect this region from being settled by the English. Both the French and the English relied on the American Indians for the fur trade and military support. Some American Indians depended on both the French and the British for trade in manufactured goods, especially weapons. All of these groups wanted to have control over the Ohio River valley. War seemed hard to avoid.

The French and Indian War

In the 1740s England gave land in the Ohio River valley to a group of colonists from Virginia. These colonists thought that they could sell parts of the Ohio wilderness to other colonists as good farmland. This land grant led to tension between the French and the English. In the early 1750s the French built forts in the Ohio River valley to secure what they felt was their territory. The British saw their claim threatened and demanded that the French remove their forts. The French refused to leave, and war soon broke out.

George Washington's battle with French forces near Fort Duquesne in 1754 is known as the Battle of Great Meadows. The battle took place near where the city of Pittsburgh, Pennsylvania, is located today. Washington's battle marked the beginning of the French and Indian War. A series of battles between the British and the French, and their American Indian allies, followed.

George Washington

Washington reads the Sunday service to his troops during the French and Indian War.

The struggle for power in North America was not the only source of conflict between Britain and France. They fought each other in Europe as well. In 1756 Britain formally declared war on France, and the Seven Years' War began. In North America the British lost many battles to the French. One of the reasons that the French were winning was their alliance with American Indians. Even though American Indians traded with both the British and the French, many American Indians believed that English colonists would force them off their land.

To help gain an advantage, both the French and the British made alliances with different American Indian groups. The two major American Indian groups involved were the Algonquians and the Iroquois. These two groups were made up of different nations that shared the same language and culture. During the French and Indian War, the French made alliances with the Algonquians and the English formed alliances with the Iroquois League. The Iroquois sided with the English partly because the Iroquois and the Algonquians had been longtime enemies.

In 1756 the war changed direction when William Pitt became Secretary of State. Pitt was a very forceful man. From London, he seized control of British forces. He appointed young generals to lead the British and colonial troops. The British forces began winning battles against the French. One of the British victories in 1758 was the capture of Fort Duquesne, the fort George Washington had failed to capture four years earlier. Washington now took part in the fort's capture.

The Iroquois joined the British side during the war. This time, the Iroquois hoped that this alliance would help them keep control of their land. The British captured Quebec, the French capital in North America, in 1759. When the British gained control of Montreal in 1760, most French territory in North America was now under British control. The war for North America between Britain and France largely ended in 1760. However, the two countries and their allies continued to fight in Europe for three more years.

William Pitt

The Treaty of Paris

The British won the French and Indian War after seven years of fighting. In 1763 the Treaty of Paris was signed, and France gave most of its claim in America to Britain, including most of Canada and all of its territory east of the Mississippi River.

England now controlled much of North America. However, the British troops and forts needed to secure his territory were too few and too far apart. Because the French were defeated and were no longer a threat, the colonists began to move west to settle. Some American Indians hoped that trade agreements could be made with the settlers, but other American Indians feared that the growing number of settlers would drive them from their lands. This movement by the colonists would have a big impact on the lives of the American Indians living in the West.

Glossary

alliance an agreement between two groups or nations to defend each other

backcountry the rugged area of land near the Appalachian Mountains

self-sufficient able to rely on oneself for most of what one needs

trading post a place where settlers and American Indians met to trade goods

tributary a stream or river that flows into a larger river